A HO

WITHIN

an anthology by

CM WRITER

Authored and illustrated by Cassandra Mackenzie Wood.

A Home Within © 2021 by
Cassandra Mackenzie Wood.

To anyone who has been taught
They are
    imperfect
    incomplete
    unworthy

Darling, you are worthy just as your are
If only you find

The home within.

———

This publication discusses themes such as mental health, depression, anxiety, body dysmorphia, and disordered eating. If you struggle with any of these topics, please considering reading this book with a trusted member of your support system.

Contents

_____

Lost - *[#9]*

Searching - *[#55]*

Found - *[#107]*

Lost

I've been avoiding it,
The voice in my head
a monster, a beast, a creature...
a child
of neglect.
Sometimes the voice rises so loud
it's the only one I hear
drowning out the rational thoughts of mine
that keep me sane (just barely).
But this child is a tragedy
repeating the only words
it's ever known,
the only ones
it's ever been taught
"you are not worthy" it screams.
as I button up my jeans
and wonder if I can find
something else to wear,
a piece of fabric to hide behind.
I oblige willingly, of course.
Does this mean I believe
my body deserves to be unseen?

- on body dysmorphia and
internalized body shame

These late night thoughts
consume me
my blood is afire
with all the lies I've ever loved.

How can I love you
when I am afraid to love myself?

I should want that, right?
And I do - but never when
I'm with you...
Never in the moment.
I can never fully let go
of the notion
that my body
if unworthy of your touch
   of your affection
   your gaze
   your love.

How can I let you
into a home
that doesn't even feel
like my own?
　　　- *intimacy*

What do you know,
as I crawl back to bed,
thinking of every time
I thought you were mine?
Tossing and turning,
"can I call you tonight?"
but you never pick up.
and I'm left in the dark.
"leave a message at the tone"
day by day
I'm growing older,
with love in my veins.

And I just wanted to say
I'm glad you found
someone.
But each step I take
feels like walking away
from a home I felt in your arms.
Stargazing
remembering the end
of that fire in our hearts,
the bitter end of young love.

Were you even real?
Were we even possible?
I guess I'll never know,
'cause you don't pick up the phone.

Perhaps we were lovers
in another life
but not this one.

      - dreaming of stranger worlds

One day I'll write a poem about
all the things you said I am,
all the things you said behind my back,
or the ones you didn't say at all,
the ones muttered through your teeth,
the ones that made me feel like I was trapped
in a body unworthy of respect
in a heart too big for this broken world
with a soul never quite feeling right.
The morning after you kissed me,
still drunk on last night's memories,
I remember what you said,
when you thought I was asleep,
when I thought we were on top of the world,
I remember you saying
you wanted to leave.

But in your departure,
I found myself.

Tear stained cheeks,
emerald eyes
staring at
the midnight sky,
you and I,
we sit in a meadow
running away from life
reminiscing of childhood's memories,
the sweetest bliss
is a double edged sword,
for in every torn love letter
is a lover who's now lost,
and in every memory of innocence,
is a child
who is no longer
soft as a babe.
They grew up.
and the world
was
harsh.

Here I am
thinking about thinking
in the small hours
of dawn
lost in dreamland
(nightmareland?)
whispers of deceit
from my own mind
drown any
twinkle of hope.
            - *fading away*

Let go.
There is magic in these dark waters,
a pathway arriving at my feet.
I am trapped.
I reach for the sky, crossing paths
with shooting stars. I pretend to
be faultless.
This is no gentle awakening.
The cool air begs me to move on
from this intoxicating moment.
Will I be awake at last?
After starting again,
Departing from the stars above.
They chant "the sun will rise again!"

But I let go of reality.
My stream of consciousness is a river
and I'm trapped in its current
beneath the surface.

There, in the eerie silence
I know the sun will rise again,
but I wonder, "will I?"

I'm not too sure what to
expect, as I tumble in slow
motion to a quick demise;
falling asleep for the last time,
and awaken for the first...

before me is a face I know well,
that has tricked me many times;
oh our dangerous flirting
between the fine line of life
and its end.

I know this time is different,
I crossed *the* line;
a one way street;
a mistake I cannot take back.

death looks at me.
silent.
"you're early."

Fear submerges my mind
like a memory
on repeat
rushing water
watch it seep
into my mouth; my soul
I can't breathe
trapped in a riptide
(don't wait for me)

Let me be.
exhale.

My thoughts
are like snakes
slivering over (and under)
my skin.

      - eating myself alive

Some days
I feel as if
I've written to my heart's content

There's nothing left
But the
Sour aftertaste
Of living up
To my past accomplishments

If only I could write
the way my mind thinks
at 3am - wide awake
and racing.

Voices fill
the spaces in between
my mind
it seems I am outnumbered
by *them*
(creatures of hate)

I begin to wonder
if it is really just me...
in here fighting
a constant battle
of lost and found
(lost and drowned)

Some days
I am convinced it is.
          - loneliness

I feel dull and repetitive. White empty noise fills my mind like days gone by. If I could escape, I would, but instead this quiet continuation of nothing runs its finger along my spine (I'm wistful for another time) when my thoughts were a garden of softly spoken poetry... not a wasteland.

Why should I write
Of happy things
Of sunsets and hope

When what I feel
Is only
Regret
Lies
Anger

I will not paint a rosy picture
For the world to look down upon
For life is not always sunshine

Another long night
of escaping
the inescapable;
I am trapped in my body.

All at once
I fall to pieces;
eyes fluttering, brain fog
stumbling like a rag doll,
collapsing in upon myself
wavering vision

And the soft thud
of the earth beneath me.
the fight is over
and I watch the clouds overhead
in peace
(in relief)

I let them transform
into something new
into arms that reach
(for me)
and I let them
take me
far
far
away
— *in dreams*

I'm afraid to write
about shame.

I guess I'm ashamed of my shame
because I preach self love
to an audience of thousands
all while
behind the screen
I tear myself
apart
to the nitty gritty
broken and hollow bits of my soul.

It is as if there's an abyss in my chest
a black hole
whispering my name
over
and over
and over.

And when I begin to think
I've let myself slip
in any way, shape, or form,

it hisses
"you are unworthy."

I gasp for oxygen
in between debilitating thoughts
that hiss and claw and
drag me beneath the
churning water
that is my mind.

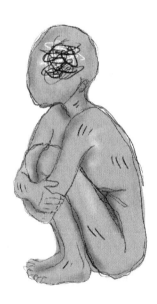

The number.

I obey to its power... cowering
(I don't want to look)

but why am I so afraid
of an arbitrary number?

why do I grant it the power
to override what I know to be true"
I am happy and energized and perfectly content.

why do I let it control me?
   - *the scale*

Just another day
of resenting
my body
and the fuel
I give it
to survive.

Looking at myself
In any mirror
Is oftentimes like looking through
A kaleidoscope,
But instead of rainbows
I see every little thing
I wish I could change.

Overthinking about everything (again). What will they think of the acne on my back? The hair on my legs? The size of my jeans? The way my stomach looks when I sit? My double chin? And every other insecurity I could ever possibly fathom.

- *I'm over it*.

How many times
will I pick myself apart
until I crumble?

I once believed
I would spend my life
endlessly chasing
the unobtainable.
    - hopeless

I don't always love myself,
sometimes the deceiving mirror
on the wall
tells me I am not
the fairest of them all;
I am unworthy
of my own love.

These mind games
deceive
trick
betray

I am a slave to its power
cowering at the sour taste
of hatred
sliding down my throat
biting back salty tears
as my enemy cheers
for my demise.

The world ignores my cries
as I submit
and the light dies.

I don't always love myself,
but I try.

Some days I feel like
another log on the fire
drifting slowly
in parallel
in a smokey yard
full of love and shades of orange
as I burn, tenderly
waking up to screaming embers
splintering bones
the howl of a fire
as I go up in flames
until I am only a few embers
above the welcoming crowd.
until I am darkness.

Where did the light go?

Nausea rolls over my mind
like a wave; pulling me under.
It seems the spinning of my mind
has given me
motion sickness.

"Just look at yourself"
time escapes
as the hidden chambers
of shame ignite
with fright and fury

I am ashamed;
and yet looking at myself
is like looking through
a kaleidoscope:
everything is distorted
(I lost track of what is real a long time ago)

so here I am
trying to tame the monsters in my head
that place me on a pedestal
to be mocked
until I collapse;
never feeling good *enough*
that perfection is *just* out of reach
one week more
trust me, they say
and I succumb another day.

If only I were more like her
    - *the words I lost myself to*

The phantom tune of a piano
wails
whistles
in the windy moor.
People run
soaked in dew
from the ruins
of a castle
that was once
a home.
Now it crumbles.
Now it is empty.
  - I am the castle

How many times have I blamed by body for being human?
How many times have I let my insecurities hold me back?

I hid my tears in the darkness.
I hid my insecurities behind a smile.
I played the part
of perfection (the unattainable)

Until
there was
nothing real
left inside.
At rock bottom I prayed
for the semblance of normality.

- I'm (not) fine

I'm not fine.
I yell
in silence
again.

never brave enough
to admit
I was not
the perfect person
I presented myself as.

I'm not fine.
I tear myself apart
for every little
non-existent flaw
that I've been taught
to change.

I'm not fine.
I'm trapped in my obsessive thoughts
if only
if only
IF ONLY...

I'm not fine.

My mind is at war with my body.
But who started this war?

Too many nights wishing upon superstars
Like shooting stars
With an empty plate
Slowly drowning in silence as I wait
As I wonder
"How many calories have I ate?"

I'm sad I'm broken again,
Lies slipping through my teeth
Like silk.
"I'm fine," I say
As guilt crawls beneath my skin.
I feel like somebody else.
Falling
In
Reverse
With a double knotted tongue
And a fake smile,
Too late (again) to take it back:
What I said to my body that day,
Who was just trying to stay alive
As I resented it for not fitting right

In those blue jeans
From the eighth grade.
I want to disappear (but please notice)
As I critique
    My every move
        Every meal
            Every mark
                Every little thing that makes me
real.
I never loved my first home
Because
I was never shown how to love it;
Only hate.

I was taught every remedy for
    Red skin
    Bloating
    Stretch marks
    (*none of which require fixing of any kind at all*)
And not the only medicine I truly needed:

Self love.

But that's not profitable to the media
So I've got none.
I've gone numb.

Stop telling me you're okay.
It's clear to me,
you
are
not.
My entire existence crumbles
because I know
when you are all alone
late at night
in the darkness,
there is no place
that you feel at home.
    - a letter to myself

Darling,
this too, shall pass.
The long night,
leads to awakening.
     - *a letter from my future self*

Searching

I am searching for
a paradise,
for a home I know exists
in my skin,
my bones,
myself.

Chaos.
It seems I can't control
the beast
inside my mind;
a creature of torment,
of pity,
of neglect.

Perhaps this monster is lost.
Perhaps this monster is afraid
      is anxious
      is defeated
      is me

To the beast inside:
let me take your hand.

"I'll meet you there"
I say
as I catch a glimpse of my reflection
passing by
like a ghost
imagining the daydream
dreamt so many times.
It feels more like a memory;
a world
where I feel beautiful.
A world where I feel
I belong.

Let go
of the sharp knife
of perfection;
the fine line
between "I'm fine"
and destruction.

Look after yourself,
because healing happens in layers,
never all at once...
and never linear.
So if you find yourself
where you started,
please remember,
it is not the same
as never leaving at all.
Embrace the quiet sense
of a journey
towards self love.

I want to hide
beneath these clothes.
I know - my body does not define
my worth.
My virtue is divine
and I won't let this doubt confine me
(although the beast inside tries).
This space I occupy is ethereal
being more does not make me less
heavenly hips
lavender lips
thunder thighs
the universe sighs.
I am soft *and* I am strong.
I am resilience.
I. Am. Worthy.

I don't thank you enough
for all that you do
for keeping me
sane
happy
healthy
alive.

     - to my body

Start with peace,
not anger.

Even today,
there are days
when I'm not quite sure
what's in my head
and what is truly real.

But I've decided that
what I see
(in the mirror or in my mind)
does not define
who I am;
does not define
my joy or passion.
I am so much more than a body.

So. Much. More.

I want to take you to the movies
To watch the film you've been going on about
For months and months.

I want to play with your hair
To watch the sunset dance in your locks
As I grin from ear to ear.

I want to write you endless love letters
To express my gratitude
In paragraphs and pages.

I want to lay my head on your shoulder,
To hear your heartbeat going strong
As peace fills my soul.

I want to feel complete
On my own.

I want to take myself out
To see the world.

You are not the problem.
Their perception of you is.

It seems I am fighting an endless battle...
of repetition and habit
creating my demise.
I fall back,
tumbling-stomach-in-throat-I-can't-breathe
as gravity escapes and I tumble
into an old pattern
of hate
of *fear* masquerading as hate.
Fear of judgement
of failure
of never being enough.
Wouldn't I feel better
if only I were smaller?

Less than.
If I reduce myself to near nothing
(skin and bones)
will I feel *enough*?
Would people really praise me
for being hollow?
A shell of myself
(that fits in size 2 jeans)

The real failure, my dear,
is believing
you are not enough
exactly as you are
    - you are enough

Stop comparing yourself to others.
The sunflower doesn't
Envy the rose.
Both have their beauty.

I was addicted to
controlling the uncontrollable;
my body
my perception of it
(despite that dysmorphia ruled my mind)
and I let this obsession
eat away at
the passion I once held for life
missing out on
meals with friends
(praying my fixation with perfection would end)
skipping summer days by the river
because I was dependant on praise.

I'm glad
I am not that girl
anymore.

It was my own judgment
the whole time.
    - internalized body shame

Some days will feel empty
and that is okay.

Some days will feel dark
and that is okay.

Some days will feel like chaos and that is okay.

It's okay
because
some days will feel
like sunshine
joy
love
fulfillment

The sun shines after the storm.

Tonight I cry
for what I really wanted
all along

I let my salty tears
fill my hollow soul
with a raging ocean,
ready to shape the shoreline
into something new.

What I really wanted
all along
was a self-love
so pure
it filled the abyss
in my mind.

I'm sorry for all the ways
I've tried to force you to change
when really
you were already
perfect
as you are
- to my body

And for the first time in what feels like forever,
I look into the mirror and smile.

What truly matters
is how you treat
yourself.

You will never find self love
if the only dialogue
you have with your body
is hate.
Instead, focus on gratitude.
Focus on what your body does for you.
Life is too short
to spend it
criticizing yourself.

Resentment is not
a good motivator.
You can't resent your existence
into a better version of yourself.
You have to love yourself
along the way;
the highs and the lows.

  - self love is the best motivator for change

Be brave enough
to water your
own garden first.

Stop shrinking yourself
to fit in the space
that pleases others.
You have outgrown it.
Instead, claim your garden.
Bloom.

worth ≠ approval
    ≠ a certain body type
    ≠ fulfilling *their* expectations

worth is how *you* define it
for yourself.

Forbidden fruit never tasted so sweet,
the apple of my eye
(you make me weak)
a goddess of love
and light and liberation
a holy being
that exists within my soul;
you make me whole
as I face the stake
of internal judgment
I tremble and shake
in the wake of past mistakes
but always are you there
the bittersweet taste,
the most royal of red
between my teeth
in my blood
my mind
my soul

If you say this is a sin,
to love yourself wholeheartedly,
forbidden fruit never tasted so sweet.

Take up all the space you need
to live your life
to its fullest.

Taking your own hand,
and embarking on the innermost journey
of self love

is like
getting lost in a book
or waking
from the sweetest of dreams.

Reflections on the windows
suddenly become meaningful,
I know who I am
in mind
in soul.

This place (my heart)
is a place I've been before
but never like this;
without judgment;
without shame;
without an ounce of expectation.

I am here for myself.

Whatever you choose to become,
you must first,
choose happy.

Find someone
who loves you for who you are
not who you could become with time
not who you could've been in another life.

Your soulmate it out there
and they will love you for
who you are now
who you have been
and who you may become
(regardless of who that may be)
         - and darling your soulmate may be yourself

There is so much out there
Waiting for someone (you)
To decide
They want to seize the day.

You cannot pour from an empty cup,
So be kind to yourself,
Let tears of joy and sorrow
Drip from your cheeks
Into the chalice
And let them
Water that deep,
Neglected garden
Within your soul
Simply waiting for some love
So it may bloom.

Your power is not defined
by your body
but by the resilience
of your heart and soul.

Some days I feel trapped
In all the
What ifs
But despite
The
Would've, could've, should've

There is always tomorrow
To *do*.

Courage and fear
go hand in hand.

It is brave to face the voice
inside your mind
commanding you
to spread hate within
(instead of love)

It is the fear of staying the same
(remaining trapped)
that inspires us
to have the courage to change.

I want to take up as much space as possible,
I want to be heard,
I want to be seen.

I don't want to hide myself away
because I deemed myself unworthy.

This is my life.
It is worth living.

Embrace stillness
and step into the divine light
that is your soul.

I look her in the eyes
and say

"it will all be okay, trust me"

- *to my past self*

Before I am a daughter
a sister
a student
a partner

I am myself.

Before I am a woman
A body to judge
An object to use

I am myself.

My concept of individuality
is not reliant
on how others
perceive me.

I am my own.

Cherish authenticity.
The most beautiful of gardens
has hundreds of flowers
each unique from the next.
What is a garden without
sunflowers, roses, tulips, and trees,
thistles, daisies, lilies, and leaves?
Darling, who you are is pure *magic*.

You will not take more from me.
All my life
I have given
and given
and given some more.

I gave you all I had
when I was at rock bottom
salt running down my cheeks
and I begged the darkness
to make me thin
(why did I never beg it to make me happy?)

But the darkness will not steal
anything else from me.
I need not beg for my inner peace
nor my joy or sanity,
I am complete.

I am happy.
And I was the one who got me here.

The sky is not the limit.
Never feel bound
By what others say
By what others
Believe you are capable of.

If you want to go to the moon,
Go to the moon.

But why stop there
If there's a whole universe
Out there
Waiting for you to see?

The future blooms
from the seeds you plant
today.

I've finally discovered
balance
between nourishing my body
and my soul,
balance
between how I feel
and how I love myself.
It is like the sweetest of
sunsets
coursing through my veins.
       - *complete bliss*

I am searching an endless sea
for a home
that has always been with me.
- *the home within*

Found

.

Only if you become lost in the woods,
do you truly get to explore it
for yourself.

But first
you have to
trust yourself.

Life is too short to spend it
criticizing yourself.
Self love is the way
to freedom.

Why should I resent you
For giving me a home?

Why should I shame you
For the stretch marks
On your thighs
Your hips
Your chest?

Why should I hide you away
For carrying me through life
With pride?

Why should I distort you,
Suck you in,
Until you can barely breathe?

You don't need to change,
And I'm sorry
For all the times I tried to
Make you anything other
Than who you were meant to.

I am healthy,
Inside and out,
Thanks to you.
                - thank you to my body

No matter who they want you to be
No matter who you think you should be

You are enough
Right now
And you are worthy
Of the life you want to live.

Before I am your goddess,
I am my own.

There is no amount of hate
That will change you
Into the person you want to be.
Only love darling, only love.

I will always search
for the ray of sunshine
the lone wildflower
the singing birds
the brightest star
and every other
little
       piece
            of
          hope.

I could write pages and pages
about night-time and how your eyes
light up in a particular colour -
but how could my words
ever do justice
to the stars and planets dazzling
like pools of moondust and sunshine?
It's almost like being underwater
staring up at the sun
rippling through
as you exhale your final ounces of oxygen
and the sweet bliss encompasses
your mind and soul.

You make me breathless.
- to my inner goddess

You are a goddess
in all that you are
in all that you've been
in all that you will become.

I used to live absently,
fraught with anger, frustration
and sorrow
directed in upon my soul
for not being *normal* enough.

But today
I celebrate my unique authenticity,
this experience of discovery
and renewal
and enlightenment
taught me to embrace who I am
to be seen
for who I am.

There's nothing more sweet
Than stumbling upon
Something so good
(A paradise)
Without even searching
(Endlessly)

I am not my thoughts
I am not my body

I am so much more.

If anything
Obsess about
Everything that brings you joy
(And not what drains you of it)

And although the tides may rise
I will hold your hand
And be the oxygen you need
To breathe

   - words I needed

Trying on last year's jeans
will not grant you validity.
That denim does not
define your worth.
You are so much more than
your insecurities.
We've been conditioned to
believe that happiness
                worth
                confidence
are all one-size commodities.

In truth,
joy only comes from liberation,
by shedding the weight...
of societal beauty standards,
of other people's judgements,
of body dysmorphia,
of our own internalized scrutiny.

Happiness is not one size fits all.
It is every size for all.

This body is a home,
not a trend
not an object
(as you may have me believe).
This body serves me.
I accept myself
as I am.

Sex and sexuality
forbidden
spoken about in silence
taboo
uncomfortable
off-limit
shameful
scandalous...

but *what if* I am curious?
and in my wonder I find power.
what if I find reclamation?

Sex is not shameful.
Sexuality is not shameful.
These things are beautiful
and powerful
and *empowering*.

Let us not shroud sex with shame.
get curious.
explore.

There is freedom in this world of intimacy.
There is power in this world of vulnerability.

Your difference is your beauty.
Your authenticity is your strength.
Beside every woman
is a community of fellow women.
Much like the stars at night,
it is far more beautiful
when we shine together.

Relearning to love yourself
is not always graceful.
But there is rebirth
in falling apart.

The most magical things
arise from embracing
your most authentic self.

I do not exist
to be *beautiful*.
I exist
to be *me*.

Darling,
have the courage to be true,
to be authentic,
to be disliked.
to be vulnerable.

Happiness awaits beyond those doors.

And all the long
winding roads
were really just
leading me back
to myself.

Your beauty is not based on
the clarity of your skin
the size of your waist
the hair on your arms.
Your worth
is not
dependant on physicality.
You are enough;
inside and out;
here and now
(and for all you may become)

Darling, your most beautiful form
Is not the
Thinnest
Smallest
Curviest
Hungriest

It is the
Happiest
Most authentic
Most energized

I will no longer value
thinness and appearance
over health and wellbeing.

I will not be reduced to my
clothing size
waistline
complexion
or composure.

I am so much more
and so are you.

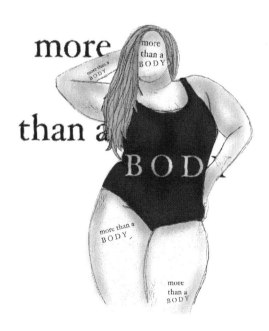

Comparing myself to others,
made me feel less beautiful.
But I have come to realize
that when we look up at the sky,
in complete awe of its vastness,
we do not compare one star
to another;
the light of one
does not diminish the other.

The cosmos are far more beautiful
when we all shine
together.

Slow down,
for there is beauty in moments
that would otherwise
slip by unnoticed;
like the sun through the trees
a birdsong in the leaves...

there is beauty in places
you may not seek to look
like laughing dimples
forehead crinkles
a belly well fed
sleeping peacefully in bed...
        - *find the beauty*

You deserve to nourish your body.
Fuel your mind and soul.
Seek movement
that brings you ease.
Remember that rest is just as productive
(if not more)
than long nights
pushing through...
to burnout.

You are worthy
of joy
of self-love
of balance.

One day I woke up
and it all felt like
a bad dream.

    - years later

If only we taught our children to love their bodies, instead of how to change them.

Chase what makes you happy
Like the butterfly rides the wind.
It doesn't have to make sense
To everyone,
But it has to inspire you
To live your best life.

Nourish your soul.

Practicing self-love
is like strengthening a muscle;
the more you use it
the stronger you get.

To the moon and back
I love you
not in spite of your craters,
not despite you are not always full,
but because.

Remember to always have patience
with life
and with others,
but most importantly
with yourself.

Never be ashamed
of yourself
be proud
be authentic
uphold your commitment
to becoming your best self
through self-love.

I may preach authenticity
in my every breath.

And
I am still insecure.
I still make mistakes.

But I am *always* worthy.
These are not faults.
They are human.

Sing your soul a lullaby,
revel in the simple joy
of lilting to the tune
of your heart's truest song.

There is no *right* way
to be beautiful.
Beauty *is* authenticity

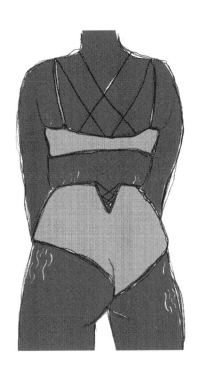

There is joy
in the simplicity of life,
where less is more,
because you savour it,
and days of nothing,
are really days of everything.
Give your heart over
to the easy life,
watch heaven sigh over you
with the sweetness of sunshine.

It is a strange feeling;
departing from what I've always known
and yet coming back
to who I've always been

The search is done;
I have found
the home within.

Acknowledgments

Thank you to my parents, for your constant love, support, and encouragement. Thank you for the countless hours you spent helping me develop, refine, and edit this project. I am eternally grateful for our 3-person editing team.

Thank you to my readers, for being advocates of my poetry, for inspiring me to be resilient, and for simply being your most authentic selves. Our poetry community truly is a beautiful thing; one of many homes I am thankful to have in my life.

And finally, thank you to all who helped me find the home within, especially when I was lost.

About the Author

CM Writer, also known as Cassandra Mackenzie Wood, is a young Canadian poet, novelist, and storyteller. Cassandra's collection includes her debut book *The Roots of a Goddess*, her second poetry compilation *Wonder of the Cosmos*, and *Paint Us Red*, an international women's empowerment anthology. Along with these works, she is committed to sharing daily poetry on her Instagram platform @CM.Writer.

With the power of her words, Cassandra hopes to spread mental health awareness and advocate for social issues that impact the world today.

Printed in Great Britain
by Amazon